Ippie

Unschooled

Written by
Nicole Olson

Illustrated by Alexis Zires

About the Artwork

The artwork in this book was done entirely by children who are homeschooled/unschooled.

Main Illustrator: Alexis Zires - age 12

Additional Artwork By:

Royce King - age 4

Topher King - age 11

Michelle Dakotah Gunton-Lamothe - age 12

Summer Cheyenne Gunton-Lamothe - age 8

Thomas J. Olson - age 10

Faith B. Olson - age 7

Katy Olson - age 7

Maggie Rebecca Olson - age 3

Eli Tripp - age 7

Odin Bae Tripp - age 5

Graphics: Tina Christopher

Cover Design: Denis Lucien

Acknowledgments

My deepest gratitude to:

My mother, Donna Puleo, whose suggestion was the spark for this story.

Erica Silvestri, who helped me find my vision when it was little more than a blur.

Sandra Zires, who worked with both Alexis and me to make this exciting collaboration possible.

Tina Christopher, whose dedication, talent, and selfless giving of her time and skill helped bring Ippie to life.

Alison Klienfeld, whose editorial skill is truly impressive.

The King family, who gave of their time, shared their home, and graciously lent me the best graphic artist out there.

Topher, Royce, and Thomas for their refreshingly honest feedback.

My husband, Ted Olson, for his encouragement and support, especially at crunch time! Words can't express my gratitude to him for all the ways he filled in to allow me the time and freedom to finish this book. I am truly blessed.

My children, Thomas, Faith, Katy, and Maggie, who take this unschooling journey with me every day. I'm so grateful for our life together!

For my children, Thomas, Faith, Katy and Maggie, who together make Ippie who she is, and for the many courageous unschooling families who strive to make this amazing philosophy better understood by those around them.

-Nicole

I would like to dedicate this book to my amazing nephew, Phoenix. Make your life a work of art and always eat your vegetables. I love you.

-Alexis

Sunlight slipped around the edges of the window shade and gently rested on Ippie's smooth, curved cheek.

"Wake up, Ippie," it seemed to whisper. "The world is waiting for you."

Ippie stretched, rubbed her eyes, and snuggled under her blankets for a moment, enjoying the quiet warmth. She slid out of bed, catching hold of her favorite pink blanket. Wrapping up tight inside it, Ippie made her way to the top of the stairs.

Curling her body into a ball, Ippie slowly rolled down the stairs, quietly squeaking with each new step. By the third one, Ippie's mother had come to greet her.

"Oh, my, it's a little pink ball rolling down the stairs! Good morning little ball!" Ippie's mom kissed her cheek through the blanket and playfully tickled her ribs.

Ippie peeked one eye out of her pink cocoon and winked at her mom. She emerged from her blanket, her arms open wide. Her mom gathered her up and carried her down to the living room, where Ippie settled onto the couch. In the kitchen she could hear her brother and sister eating breakfast.

"You slept in today, Ippie," said her mom. "You must be feeling great. There's nothing like a good night's sleep!"

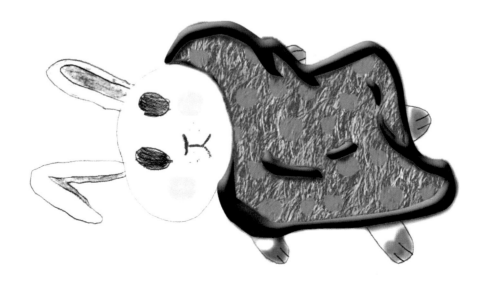

Ippie nodded and padded into the kitchen. Her mother set down a glass of water - Ippie hated juice - and her favorite purple plate. Ippie helped herself to a freshly baked muffin and some fruit.

While she munched, she listened as her brother practiced lines for their play.

"Ippie, read your lines for me, will you?" he asked.

Ippie slid her chair next to her brother's and looked at the script. He pointed out the lines he wanted her to read, and as she nibbled her muffin, she followed along.

"Jamie, what's *k-n-o-w* spell?" Ippie asked, coming to an unfamiliar word.

"Let me see," Jamie replied. "Oh, that's *know*. The *k* at the beginning is silent."

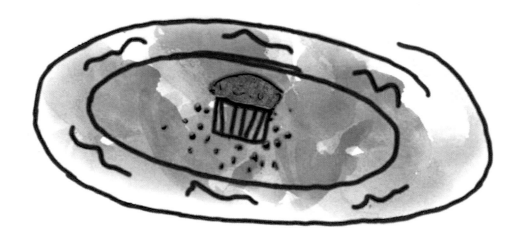

When they had finished practicing, Ippie slipped into her clothes and brushed her teeth.

"All set?" asked her mom.

"All set!" Ippie ran upstairs to find her colored pencils. "Don't want to forget these!" she said to herself as she raced back down the stairs.

Just as she reached the bottom, Ippie's little sister summoned her.

"Can you help me log into email?" asked Becky.

Ippie showed Becky how to move the mouse and type in the password.

"Now hit enter," Ippie instructed, scanning over the inbox. She clicked on a message from their British friend, Ruby.

"What does it say, Ippie?"

"It says that Ruby is going to Skype us tomorrow at 4:00

p.m. her time. Let's see, that makes it..." Ippie did some quick calculating, "9:00 a.m. our time. Cool! I can't wait to talk to her!"

Ippie heard her brother opening the front door.

"Wait for me!" she yelled. "Mom, can I wait for the school bus outside?"

"Sure, honey," her mother called back. "It'll be here in a bit. Half day today, right?"

Ippie skipped out the door and hurried over to her brother. He was kneeling down, looking at something by the tree.

"Look! A nest!" Jamie exclaimed.

A tiny nest had fallen from the tree. Nestled inside was a single, brightly colored feather. Ippie snatched the feather up and tucked it into her pocket. It would be a great addition to her feather collection. Later, she and her mom would study it under the microscope, then try to identify it with the bird book that was always handy.

As she turned away from the nest, she noticed something strange. There was a sizable lump pushing up the grass. The lump was about as big around as Ippie's hula hoop. She bent down to get a closer look. Hundreds - maybe thousands - of ants were busily entering and exiting. Some were carrying food in, others hauling bits of dirt out. Ippie was fascinated.

"Jamie, come here! You won't believe this ant hill I found. I'm going to get the magnifying glasses!" Ippie zipped back into the house, grabbed two magnifying glasses, and ran back out to inspect the ants. She and Jamie watched them intently.

"Let's help the ants get more food!" Ippie exclaimed. Jamie found a bit of carrot from the compost heap and placed it near the ants. They watched as the insects swarmed around and over it.

"Let's try something else!" suggested Jamie. Soon a crust of bread, a crumb from the cookie jar, and a stale potato chip joined the carrot. Jamie and Ippie closely observed, eager to see which food turned out to be the most popular.

"It's going to be the cookie crumb," predicted Jamie. "Ants love sweet things."

When they were finished watching the ants, Ippie and Jamie decided to have scooter races up and down their long driveway. Jamie had longer legs, but Ippie's scooter had more zip. Finally tired, Ippie sat down on the driveway, picked up a piece of colored chalk and began to draw.

"What are you making?" Jamie asked.

"A castle. Want to help?" Ippie replied.

Soon the two of them had created an entire kingdom filled with forests, lakes, farms, and towns. They drew lanes and used their model horses to ride through the kingdom, protecting it from evil sorcerers and the dragon that lurked just over the northernmost mountain.

A screen door banged. Looking up, Ippie spotted their elderly neighbor, Mrs. Jones.

"How are my little friends today?" Mrs. Jones called to them. "Come on over here; I've got something for you."

Ippie and Jamie scurried next door to see what it was. Mrs. Jones handed Ippie a sandwich baggie containing several coins.

"I found these yesterday tucked way back in my closet," Mrs. Jones explained. "I thought you two might like to have them."

"What are they?" Ippie asked her. "That doesn't look like real money."

"Oh, it's real alright. This money comes from another country. My husband brought it home after the war."

Ippie and Jamie hadn't known Mr. Jones had been in a war. They wanted to hear all about it. Mrs. Jones motioned for them to sit with her on the porch swing, and as they rocked, she told them stories about her husband's travels during the Second World War. Ippie and Jamie were spellbound.

After Mrs. Jones went back inside, Ippie and Jamie dashed home.

"Mom!" Ippie called out. "Can you help me look up Germany? I want to see where it is."

Ippie's mother joined her at the computer. A few moments later they had printed out a map of Europe.

Just then, they heard the rumbling sound of the school bus. Ippie grabbed her colored pencils, threw them into her bag, and darted out the door.

"Bye, Mom!" she sang.

Ippie walked next door to her friend Emma's house. She waited until the bus came to a stop. The doors opened, and Emma emerged.

"Hi, Emma!" said Ippie, "Are you ready for our play date? I brought the colored pencils to decorate the paper dolls."

"Hi, Ippie!" Emma answered. "Sure I'm ready. I've been dying to get home and get started!"

Ippie and Emma meandered toward Emma's house, chatting.

"What did you do at school today, Emma?" asked Ippie.

"Mmmm...we had a spelling test," Emma replied, "and we played a math game. We cleaned out our desks, and we worked on writing paragraphs."

"What was your favorite part?" Ippie inquired.

"Recess!" Emma exclaimed happily.

"What did you do today, Ippie? Did your mother give you spelling words?" asked Emma.

"No," said Ippie.

"Did you have to practice your math facts?"

"No," said Ippie.

"Well, what about worksheets? Didn't you have any worksheets to finish?"

"No," said Ippie.

"You mean you didn't have to learn anything again today?"

Ippie thought back over her morning...

Emma interrupted her thought. "You're so lucky you don't have to go to school. Homeschooling seems like so much fun!"

"I'm unschooled," said Ippie.

"Unschooled?" Emma repeated, confused.

"Yeah, unschooled. It means you learn just by living. My mom says that when you're busy doing what you love, the whole world is your classroom. And you're right, Emma, it is really fun!"

The End

Notes from Ippie's Mom

Welcome, everyone! Now that you've had a glimpse of Ippie's morning, I want to give you a "behind the scenes" look into my role in the unschooling journey of my children.

Although unschooling is child-driven, it is far from hands-off. My role is to closely observe and engage in the interests and inclinations of my children. I provide a wealth of materials, experiences and opportunities to support and extend those interests. Here are a few examples of unschooling in action.

My son Jamie is very interested in theater. I've supported that interest by finding local theater productions to attend together and by enrolling him in children's theater workshops. I borrowed library books about playwriting and helped Jamie type scripts for plays he's written. I also work with him to learn lines and give him feedback on his delivery.

To support Ippie's love of birds, I keep guides easily accessible, and help her identify distinguishing characteristics of varying species. We created a chart of birds we see in our yard, and are planning to participate in The Great Backyard Bird Count, an annual event that engages bird watchers of all ages in counting birds.

Becky is really drawn to fashion design and sewing, so I spend time helping her with projects, making all kinds of creations from scraps of fabric and old clothes. I've also connected her to a family friend who is a sewing enthusiast. In addition, we watch a television series that depicts the creative process of fashion design.

And that's just the tip of the iceberg!

As my children encounter new and interesting ideas, I look for ways to allow them to engage more deeply. For example, after today's conversation with Mrs. Jones, Ippie and Jamie may want to know more about World War II. I went through our books and pulled out several historical fiction chapter books that are set in that time period. Later on, I'll mention them to Ippie and Jamie and offer to read with them. If their interest continues, I'll find other ways to help them discover more.

As an unschooling parent, I need to be aware of each child's learning style and preference. While Ippie and Jamie tend to approach learning in a very hands-on, experiential way, Becky really enjoys a more methodical approach. When there's a skill she wants to master, she is drawn to more formal curriculum and skill-specific worksheets, which I am happy to provide for her.

Parents can feel intimidated by unschooling, because they worry that they couldn't teach their child. But it's not so much a matter of knowing how to *teach* your children; it's about *engaging* with your children - following their passions and sharing your own. Unschooling is a dynamic, exciting approach which has brought my family closer together while expanding our horizons.

What Did Ippie Learn?

Curious about all the learning that took place during Ippie's morning? You might be surprised to discover the many important skills embedded within Ippie's activities. Take a look...

Ippie and Jamie practicing the script

Subject Areas: English Language Arts, Performing Arts

Skills: decoding, reading for meaning, reading aloud, reading with emotion, public speaking, theater-related vocabulary and technical terms, working with a peer

Ippie and Becky on the computer

Subject Areas: English Language Arts, Mathematics, Technology, Social Studies, Socialization

Skills: decoding, composing, mental mathematics, subtraction, computer programs and applications, world geography, time zones, cross-cultural studies, developing multi-age relationships, peer tutoring

Ippie and Jamie outside

Subject Areas: Science, Physical Education, Visual Arts, English Language Arts, Social Studies, Socialization

Skills: life science, scientific method, aerobic movement, creating large scale drawings, working collaboratively, storytelling, geography, cross-cultural studies, history, interviewing a witness to historical events, developing multi-generational relationships

Ippie and her mom

Subject Areas: Social Studies, Technology

Skills: world geography, methods of research/finding information

Ippie and Emma

Subject Areas: Socialization, Civics

Skills: developing friendships, working collaboratively, exposure to different points of view

What is Unschooling?

Simply put, unschooling is a form of homeschooling. It is legal throughout the United States. It is practiced world-wide, and is growing rapidly as more and more families find themselves dissatisfied with traditional education systems.

Unschooling can be described as a child-led, adult-supported, passion-based way of life. It is rooted in the idea that children are natural learners, filled with curiosity about the world around them. It takes into account the fact that children develop at different rates, and vary greatly in their learning styles. The unschooling philosophy asserts that exploring one's interests is profoundly meaningful and produces deep, enduring learning.

To learn more about unschooling, visit Nicole Olson's website: www.unschoolers.org

Unschooling in Real Life

The publishing of this book is an excellent example of unschooling in action.

Once I finished writing Ippie Unschooled, I began looking for an illustrator. After considering several professionals, I had an inspiration: why not find an unschooler?

I reached out to the unschooling community, and connected with Alexis Zires, a twelve-year-old self-taught artist. She completely captured the essence of Ippie, and our collaboration began.

Alexis' mother worked with us, offering Alexis feedback, scanning and sending drawings, and keeping in touch with me. Soon Alexis' sketches were complete. Next step: bringing the art and text together.

Once again, I reached out to the unschooling community, this time in need of a graphic artist. That's how I found Tina Christopher, who not only embraced my vision, but expanded on it. She suggested we invite kids from our homeschooling community to contribute art. Soon we had pictures from ten children!

As Tina digitized and placed the artwork, she included my children and her own in the process, showing them how to add color to their creations and getting their feedback about each page as it developed. It was inspiring to witness their enthusiasm as the book began to come together!

And the opportunities for learning continue! Alexis collects a share of the royalties, and is learning how to use the publisher's tracking and sales software to calculate her earnings. My son, Thomas, has developed confidence in his artistic skill, and is currently illustrating the second book in the Ippie series. Tina and I have been invited to speak to a group of homeschoolers about the process of writing and publishing a book.

The multi-age collaboration, the many academic skills embedded in the process, and the real-life experience of bringing a book to life made this a truly meaningful experience to all involved - adults and children alike. That's the magic of unschooling in action

Made in the USA
Monee, IL
24 November 2024

71067858R00024